Original title:

The Heart's Path

Copyright © 2024 Creative Arts Management OÜ

Author: Levi Montgomery
ISBN HARDBACK: 978-9916-90-772-6
ISBN PAPERBACK: 978-9916-90-773-3

Threads Woven in Silent Vows

In twilight's grace, we make our vows,
Silent whispers, where love allows.
Each thread entwined, a story spun,
In the quiet bliss, two hearts are one.

With every stitch, a promise wears,
In the fabric of life, a tapestry shares.
Through storms and calm, our bonds will stay,
Woven together, come what may.

Bridges Over Troubled Waters

Across the waves, a bridge of hope,
Together we rise, together we cope.
Through tempest's roar, hand in hand we stand,
Facing the tides, a united band.

Beneath the surface, our fears may hide,
Yet love's resilience shall be our guide.
With each step forward, the path we pave,
A journey to cherish, a heart that's brave.

Footprints in the Sand of Time

Footprints left on the sandy shore,
Tales of the past, of dreams we wore.
Waves wash away, yet memories stay,
In the golden glow of the ending day.

Each step a whisper, each grain a story,
Marking the journey in fleeting glory.
As tides of time ebb and flow,
In the heart's archive, love will grow.

The Garden of Fragile Whispers

In a garden where secrets bloom,
Whispers of petals dispel the gloom.
With every breath, a scent so sweet,
Nature's embrace, a tranquil retreat.

Among the blossoms, dreams take flight,
Fragile hopes bask in soft sunlight.
In this haven where time stands still,
The heart finds solace, the soul does thrill.

Secrets Beneath the Surface

Whispers dance in twilight's glow,
Beneath the waves, where shadows flow.
Hidden tales, in silence lie,
Veiled in dreams, they softly sigh.

In depths where no light dares to creep,
Ancient stories, secrets keep.
Glimmers fade in twilight's haze,
Eternal dances charm our days.

Endless Circles of Yearning

Round and round the heart does race,
Chasing echoes, lost in space.
Yearning whispers fill the night,
Fueling flames that burn so bright.

In the stillness, hopes compose,
Woven threads of dreams and prose.
Circles spin with every sigh,
Binding earth and endless sky.

A Quest for Hidden Treasures

Maps of gold in crumbled hands,
Charting paths through distant lands.
Every step, a tale unfolds,
In the search for gems untold.

Secrets buried, waiting, still,
Ancient echoes, hearts to fill.
With the dawn, the journey starts,
Guided by our daring hearts.

Flux of Feelings' Passage

Like rivers twist and turn away,
Feelings flow, then fade to gray.
Moments linger, rise, and fall,
Echoes in the silent hall.

Shifting sands beneath our feet,
Heartbeats echo, soft and sweet.
In the flux of night and day,
Emotions lead us, come what may.

Sails Caught in a Southerly Wind

The sails are full, the ship takes flight,
With whispers of dreams in the soft moonlight.
Rolling waves call, a song so true,
Adventure awaits in skies of blue.

The wind wraps tightly, a lover's kiss,
Guiding us onward, to places of bliss.
Stars overhead, a map on the sea,
In this vast ocean, we are forever free.

The Compass of Intuition's Embrace

Hidden truths lie within our core,
A compass guiding to distant shores.
Feelings arise like a gentle tide,
In the heart's quiet, wisdom will bide.

We navigate life with eyes closed tight,
In dreams and whispers, we find our light.
Trust in the pull, let it lead the way,
To the dawn of hope in each new day.

Streams Flowing Toward Tomorrow

Beneath the trees, the streams babble low,
With secrets of journeys they long to show.
Rippling echoes of what's yet to be,
Carving the path through both land and sea.

In their swift rush, they dance and they flow,
Bringing forth treasures where wildflowers grow.
Each drop reflects a dream's gentle sigh,
A promise of futures that dance in the sky.

Lanterns of Night's Quiet Confessions

In the stillness, lanterns glow bright,
Casting shadows that soften the night.
Whispers of secrets float on the breeze,
As stars flicker softly, a calm to appease.

The moon listens close to the tales we share,
Of hopes and wishes, floating on air.
Each flickering flame, a story untold,
In the heart of darkness, their warmth we hold.

Embracing the Unseen

In shadows deep, we find the light,
A whisper soft, a dream in flight.
The world concealed in veils of grace,
We turn our gaze, to seek its face.

With every turn, new paths arise,
In hidden realms, the magic lies.
We learn to dance on threads of fate,
Embracing all, let love create.

Pathways of Love's Echo

Through winding roads where echoes flow,
Each step we take, love's river grows.
A melody of hearts entwined,
In every pulse, a truth we find.

Underneath the stars we tread,
With whispered dreams, our souls are fed.
In every glance, a promise stays,
Pathways formed in golden rays.

Beneath the Rhythm's Veil

The heartbeat drums, a soft embrace,
In quiet spaces, we find our place.
With every note, our spirits rise,
Beneath the rhythm, love never lies.

A dance of shadows, we adore,
In soulful tunes, we seek for more.
Together lost, we sway and spin,
In harmony, where dreams begin.

Treading on Tender Memories

Upon the path of dreams once shared,
We tread with care, our hearts laid bare.
In whispers soft, the past awakes,
With every step, the memory breaks.

Through laughter's trace and teardrops glow,
In fragile moments, love will grow.
We treasure time, both sweet and sore,
Treading on memories, we explore.

Chasing Shadows of Affection

In the twilight glow we roam,
Whispers echo like sweet foam.
Hearts entwined in dawn's embrace,
Fleeting moments, time won't erase.

Softest smiles beneath the stars,
Chasing dreams from afar.
With each glance, the silence hums,
Love's true melody becomes.

Fingers trace the dreams we've spun,
In the shadows, two as one.
Every heartbeat holds a clue,
In this dance, I'm lost in you.

The Road of Tender Encounters

Winding paths where we first met,
Every step, a sweet duet.
Gentle breezes carry sighs,
Beneath the ever-changing skies.

Laughter mingles with the leaves,
In the moment, our heart believes.
Footprints left on dusty trails,
Stories told in whispered tales.

Through the valleys, across the hills,
Sharing dreams that time fulfills.
With each turn, my heart confides,
In your gaze, the world abides.

Lanterns Lighting the Way

When the night falls, lanterns glow,
Guiding us where dreams flow.
With each flicker, hopes ignite,
In the dark, you are my light.

Candles flicker, hearts align,
In this moment, love's design.
Holding close our whispered fears,
Every tear fuels our years.

Through the shadows, we embark,
With your love, I find my spark.
Together, chasing what we've found,
In each heartbeat's sacred sound.

In Pursuit of Starlit Promises

Underneath the starlit skies,
We chase dreams, no goodbyes.
Every wish upon a star,
Guides us to who we are.

Promises like constellations,
Whispering of our aspirations.
With every hope, our spirits soar,
Together, we forever explore.

Hand in hand, through night's embrace,
In each other, we find grace.
Starlit paths, a love that's true,
In this journey, just me and you.

Glimpses Beyond the Horizon

Beneath the vast and painted sky,
Waves crash with secrets, truth, and sighs.
Where dreams are woven, fate takes flight,
Whispers of dawn, embracing the night.

Through misty valleys, shadows dance,
Each step forward, a fragile chance.
Glimpses of what could ever be,
Lurking just beyond the sea.

Words Whispers in Silence

In quiet corners, thoughts collide,
Silent words where feelings hide.
A gentle breeze, the heart's soft plea,
Lingering softly like a melody.

Between the lines of what is said,
Unspoken truths weave where we tread.
In the hush, our souls ignite,
Whispers echoing through the night.

Found in the Stronghold of Connection

In the embrace of silent trust,
Hearts alight, we soar, we must.
Bound together by unseen ties,
In the stronghold, love never lies.

Through storms and shadows, we will stand,
Holding tightly, hand in hand.
Within the depths, our spirits shine,
In this fortress, your heart is mine.

Crescendo of Hearts Uniting

With every heartbeat, music swells,
Creating magic, love compels.
A symphony of souls entwined,
In harmony, our lives aligned.

As melodies rise, we lose control,
In the crescendo, we find our role.
Together we dance, lost in the night,
In this unison, we feel the light.

Serenade of Vows in Moonlight

Underneath the silver glow,
Whispers of love softly flow.
Promised hearts in gentle dance,
Fortunes forged in whispered chance.

Beneath the stars, our secrets lie,
Eternity, our silent sigh.
With every vow, a sweet command,
In moonlit dreams, we take our stand.

Night wraps us in velvet hues,
With every gaze, the world renews.
Bound by love, a perfect rhyme,
Together, we conquer time.

The Unraveled Map of Connection

Scattered paths where shadows play,
Threads of fate along the way.
Every turn, a story told,
In the weave, connections unfold.

Pinpoints inked on canvas vast,
Memories of a shared past.
Navigating through the mist,
Every heartbeat, a promise kissed.

Winds of change may shift the course,
Yet together, we find our force.
With every step, the world aligns,
In the patterns love defines.

Echoing Valleys of Forgotten Love

Whispers lost in ancient trees,
Carried softly by the breeze.
Footsteps echo, time stands still,
In the valleys, hearts will thrill.

Lost memories paint the sky,
Echoes of a long goodbye.
Crimson leaves fall as we trace,
Every moment we embrace.

The river's song, a haunting tune,
Beneath the watchful, silver moon.
Though forgotten, love will stay,
In the heart, it finds a way.

Threads of Fate Intertwined

In the loom of life we stand,
Woven tight, hand in hand.
Every thread a tale to tell,
In the fabric, our hearts dwell.

Strands of laughter, tears, and peace,
In this tapestry, we find release.
Patterns born from joyous hopes,
Binding souls with slender ropes.

Through woven paths, we shall tread,
Embracing dreams as we are led.
In the dance of fate's embrace,
We find our home, our sacred space.

In Search of Warmth in Shadows

In the corners where light fades,
Whispers of hope begin to bloom.
Each shadow carries a tale,
Lost dreams wrapped in silent gloom.

The chill bites at tender skin,
Yet sparks of courage softly glow.
Amidst the dark, a flicker shines,
Guiding hearts where love may flow.

The Compass of Yearning

A heartbeat echoes through the night,
Direction found in longing's kiss.
With every pulse, a story calls,
A map carved from the depths of bliss.

Stars align in whispers rare,
Navigating through desires deep.
Each heartbeat leads where love must go,
In dreams, the compass wakes from sleep.

Steps on the Canvas of Emotion

Colors blend, a swirling dance,
Each step a brush, a stroke of fate.
Feelings bleed upon the page,
Creating art in love's sedate.

Footprints trace where hearts have been,
In hues of joy, in shades of pain.
Every layer tells a truth,
Life's masterpiece, a vivid chain.

Navigating Through Echoes of Care

In the stillness where love breathes,
Echoes linger, soft and clear.
With every whisper shared in trust,
Moments crafted, held quite dear.

Guided by the hearts we touch,
Through the storms, through calm and strife.
Each echo speaks of bonds we weave,
A testament to love's great life.

Unwritten Journeys of the Soul

Footsteps trace a path unknown,
Whispers of dreams in twilight's glow.
Each step a tale yet to be spun,
Navigating stars when day is done.

Winds carry thoughts of where to roam,
A heart unbound seeks its own home.
Paths diverge in the depths of night,
Awaiting dawn, a new insight.

Voices echo beneath the stars,
Mapping roads that lead to scars.
With every turn, a lesson learned,
In silence, the flame of hope burned.

Time may fade but spirits rise,
Chasing horizons, beyond the skies.
Journeys written in the soul's own ink,
In every step, we find the link.

Sculpting Memories in Silence

In quiet corners, shadows play,
Carving moments that drift away.
Hands shape the air, a gentle brush,
Each memory held in the hush.

Eyes closed tight, a world unfolds,
Stories whispered, secrets told.
Molding time with each breath drawn,
In silence, the heart's song is born.

Fragments linger, soft as light,
Captured echoes in the night.
Chiseled thoughts in stillness found,
A gallery of feelings profound.

Glass frames hold tales yet to speak,
Silent sculptures, strong but weak.
Frozen in time, yet forever flows,
A tapestry of life that glows.

Landscapes of Emotional Resonance

Mountains stand tall, shadows cast,
Echoes of emotions drifting past.
Rivers of sorrow, streams of joy,
Nature's canvas, each heart's toy.

Fields of laughter, whispers of pain,
Colors blend in the gentle rain.
Hills of trust rise, valleys of fear,
In every peak, a truth draws near.

Sunsets cradle what words can't say,
Brush strokes of twilight mark the way.
In the silence, feelings collide,
Landscapes bloom where hearts reside.

Waves of memory crash and break,
Creating shores where dreams awake.
Through every swirl, a path is shown,
In this vast world, we're never alone.

Harmony Found in Dissonance

Among the chaos, a tune emerges,
A dance between light and shadows' fringes.
Notes clash and blend, creating strife,
In discord, we discover life.

Chords intertwined, both sharp and sweet,
Rhythms of struggle guide our feet.
Melodies woven in threads of pain,
From dissonance comes the refrain.

Voices rise in a tempest's roar,
Harmony found on a distant shore.
Through the wreckage, beauty reigns,
In every clash, a soul contains.

With every tear, a story spun,
Finding solace when day is done.
In the discord, love's song still sings,
A harmony born from the wildest flings.

Vows Woven in Twilight

In twilight's glow, we softly speak,
Whispers of love, the hearts we seek.
Under stars that gently gleam,
Our promises wrapped in a dream.

With fingers entwined, we find our way,
Each vow a spark, at the close of day.
We carve our names in shadows cast,
A tapestry of futures vast.

In the quiet dusk, our hopes arise,
Reflecting truth in each other's eyes.
Bound by the magic of the night,
Our vows take wing, in shared delight.

Unfolding the Mosaic of Us

Pieces of laughter, colors unfold,
In this mosaic, our stories told.
Each memory shines, each moment bright,
Crafting our journey, a beautiful sight.

Together we gather, fragments of time,
In the dance of our lives, a perfect rhyme.
Layers of trust, a foundation strong,
In the heart of our love, we both belong.

Every fragment and hue, we embrace,
With every brushstroke, we find our place.
Through trials and joys, the image grows,
In the art of our love, the beauty flows.

Along the Streams of Emotion

We wander rivers, deep and wide,
Flowing gently, side by side.
Echoes of laughter, whispers of tears,
Carving paths through our hopes and fears.

Each bend we meet, a lesson learned,
In the currents, our passion burned.
With every ripple, we share our dreams,
Navigating life in flowing streams.

In still moments, we find our peace,
Letting love's tide offer release.
Along these waters, our spirits soar,
Together forever, we seek and explore.

Lanterns Guiding in the Dark

In shadows deep, we hold the light,
With lanterns aglow, we brave the night.
Each flicker a promise, steady and bright,
Guiding our hearts, through dark to sight.

With every step, our fears take flight,
In the glow of our love, we find our might.
Together we wander, hand in hand,
Illuminated paths, beautifully planned.

Through storms and shadows, we will roam,
Each lantern a beacon, leading us home.
In the darkest hours, love's flame will spark,
Forever united, we conquer the dark.

A Dance of Echoing Beats

In shadows where whispers play,
The heart finds its own way.
Each step beats to a tune,
Beneath a watchful moon.

Eyes meet in secret grace,
Lost in a timeless space.
A symphony unfolds,
As the night gently molds.

Fingers brush, a fleeting spark,
Lighting up the dark.
In rhythms soft and sweet,
Two souls begin to greet.

With every twist and turn,
The fires of passion burn.
Life dances in retreat,
To the echoing beats.

The Rhythm of Uncharted Emotions

In the silence of the dawn,
New feelings gently spawn.
Like waves crashing ashore,
They call for something more.

A heartbeat out of sync,
On the edge, we stand and think.
Exploring uncharted seas,
Where souls drift with the breeze.

With every rise and fall,
We listen to the call.
Threads of doubt intertwine,
Yet hope begins to shine.

Through whispers and soft sighs,
We paint the endless skies.
Emotions come alive,
In the rhythm we thrive.

Crossroads of Unspoken Truths

At the crossroads where we stand,
Silent wishes, dreams unplanned.
Words unspoken hang in air,
Promises made, but where's the care?

The tension wraps like vine,
Drawing close across the line.
Hearts yearn for what is real,
Yet hesitate to reveal.

In shadows cast by doubt,
We wander, figuring out.
Each path veiled in twilight hue,
Concealing what we knew.

But with courage, let's explore,
The truths behind the door.
In the light that breaks through,
We'll find what's tried and true.

Tides of Longing and Release

The tide pulls at our feet,
With every ebb, a retreat.
Longing fills the salty air,
As waves dance without a care.

In the stillness of the night,
Dreams take flight, hearts feel light.
Yet in the depths, a sigh,
A gentle whisper, and a cry.

As the moon weaves its spell,
We find peace within the swell.
Letting go of what confines,
In the ocean, fate aligns.

Release as dawn appears,
Washing away old fears.
In the current's sweet embrace,
We find our destined place.

Revealing the Tapestry of Belonging

Threads of stories woven tight,
Colors blend in soft twilight.
Hand in hand, we find our place,
In each heart, a warm embrace.

Whispers of laughter, joy, and tears,
Echo through the passing years.
From diverse paths, we weave our fate,
In the fabric of love, we resonate.

Roots entwined beneath the ground,
In shared moments, hope is found.
Every stitch tells who we are,
Together, we shine like a star.

Weaving dreams from every heart,
In this tapestry, we're a part.
Side by side, let's journey on,
In our belonging, we are strong.

Whispers of the Soul's Journey

The road is long, my feet are bare,
With every step, I shed my care.
Whispers guide me through the night,
Stars above, my guiding light.

In the silence, secrets dwell,
Stories waiting, hearts to tell.
Each moment a gentle breath,
In this dance, I find my depth.

Footprints left on sandy shores,
Echoing old and distant lore.
Every choice, a thread to weave,
In the tapestry of what we believe.

In the void, I find my core,
The open sky, a wide-open door.
A journey marked by love's sweet tune,
Whispers carry me to the moon.

Echoes of Desire's Trail

In the shadows, secrets sigh,
Desire burns like stars up high.
A longing glance, a whispered dream,
In tangled thoughts, we find our theme.

Every heartbeat speaks your name,
In twilight's spark, there's no shame.
Passion dances in soft light,
With every breath, we chase the night.

Hands like fire, hearts collide,
In the darkness, where dreams abide.
Each moment lingers, sweet and rare,
In this echo, love we share.

Together we explore the night,
Navigating every flight.
In the silence, desires sing,
An endless chase of everything.

Navigating Love's Labyrinth

In corridors of sweet delight,
We weave through day, we blend with night.
Twists and turns, our hearts embrace,
In the maze, we find our place.

Every path a choice we make,
In every smile, we softly wake.
Lost and found in tender sighs,
Love's bright map, a sweet surprise.

Hand in hand, we share the quest,
Finding hope within our rest.
In this labyrinth, we're entwined,
With every heartbeat, love is blind.

As we wander, time stands still,
Chasing dreams, we seek and thrill.
With each turn, our spirits soar,
In love's labyrinth, we want more.

Mapping the Terrain of Affection

In valleys where heartbeats dwell,
A river of moments, we can tell.
Mountains rise with hidden sighs,
Each peak a whisper that softly flies.

Through fields of laughter, we wander free,
Tracing the lines of you and me.
The map unfolds with every glance,
Guiding our souls in a sacred dance.

We discover paths less traveled by,
In secret corners where shadows lie.
Every touch a new landmark defined,
Together we chart what love has aligned.

With stars as our compass, we find our way,
Navigating dreams as night turns to day.
In the terrain of affection, we roam,
Creating a tapestry, stitching our home.

Echoes of Unspoken Promises

In the silence where words don't tread,
Lies a promise that lingers instead.
Beneath the stillness, our hearts reside,
In whispered vows that cannot hide.

Fleeting moments dance in the dark,
Each glance a flicker, an unlit spark.
The air is thick with dreams unsaid,
In the echoes of hopes, love's thread is wed.

Through the passages of time's embrace,
We trace the lines of our sacred space.
With every heartbeat, the truth revealed,
In unspoken promises, our souls are healed.

With every sigh, a story unfolds,
In the silence, a warmth that holds.
The echoes linger, softly embossed,
In the fabric of love, we find what's lost.

Beneath the Surface of Sweet Whispers

In shadows cast by soft moonlight,
Whispers flutter in the gentle night.
Words like petals drift and sway,
Beneath the surface, where secrets lay.

With every sigh, a truth unfolds,
In tender tones, our hearts are bold.
Silken threads entwine our souls,
As sweet whispers reveal our roles.

The currents flow beneath the skin,
In quiet moments, we let love in.
Each secret shared is a soft embrace,
Beneath the whispers, we find our place.

In the quiet, our souls ignite,
As the world fades into the night.
With every whisper, we dive deep,
Beneath the surface, our love we keep.

The Labyrinth of Intimacy

In the maze of hearts, we lose our way,
Twisting paths where shadows play.
Every turn a silent plea,
In this labyrinth, just you and me.

Walls whisper secrets of days gone by,
With every corner, we learn to fly.
A dance of souls entwined in grace,
In this complex and sacred space.

With every heartbeat, we carve our truth,
In the echoes of wonder, we find our youth.
The threads connecting our hands so tight,
Guide us through the labyrinth's light.

In the journey, we find our trust,
Navigating this bond is a must.
Together we wander, hand in hand,
In the labyrinth of intimacy, we stand.

The Unwritten Language of Desire

In whispers of the moonlit night,
Hearts beat softly, minds take flight.
The glances shared, the fleeting sighs,
In silence echoes our true ties.

A touch can speak, a brush of hands,
No words are needed for our plans.
The yearning glows in every stare,
A secret world, a love laid bare.

Through dreams we dance, though worlds apart,
An unwritten code binds each heart.
With every pulse, the fire grows,
In tender moments, desire flows.

Two souls entwined, like vines they climb,
In this language, lost in time.
Each heartbeat hints, our souls conspire,
To forge a bond through unspent fire.

Footprints in the Garden of Longing

Among the petals softly laid,
Footprints linger, love portrayed.
Each step a mark on fragrant ground,
A journey where our hearts are bound.

Beneath the arch of blooming trees,
We wander through this gentle breeze.
The softest sighs, the sweetest sounds,
In this garden, love surrounds.

With every bloom, a memory grows,
The path of longing gently flows.
In shadows cast by fading light,
Our dreams merge in the tender night.

In every rustle of the leaves,
A promise whispered, heart believes.
Together here, amidst the sighs,
Footprints vanish, but love never dies.

Threads Connecting Souls

Invisible threads weave through the air,
Connecting us beyond despair.
With every glance, the fibers tight,
In the tapestry, we find our light.

Each word we share, a stitch unspun,
The fabric grows, two become one.
With silent tales our souls are told,
In warm embrace, we break the cold.

Across the miles, the threads remain,
Through joy and sorrow, love's refrain.
In every heartbeat, the threads resound,
A bond unbroken, forever found.

As seasons change and time moves on,
These threads endure, our spirits drawn.
In the loom of life, we intertwine,
With threads of love, our souls align.

Bridges Built from Affection

In every smile, a bridge we find,
A span connecting heart and mind.
Each gentle word, a stone we lay,
Building paths to light our way.

Hand in hand, we traverse the span,
Through laughter shared, our journeys plan.
With every step, the bond we forge,
Together strong, we won't diverge.

The storms may come, the winds may rove,
Yet on this bridge, our love will prove.
With patience, trust, and sweet embrace,
We stand united, face to face.

In every sunset, every dawn,
These bridges stand, our fears are gone.
Affection's strength shall lead us home,
In love's embrace, we are not alone.

The Compass Rose of Affinity

In twilight's glow, our paths entwine,
With whispers soft, our hearts align.
The compass points to love's embrace,
In every glance, we find our place.

Through winding roads, we journey far,
The map is drawn, beneath one star.
Hand in hand, we chart the way,
In unity, we'll never sway.

With every turn, new dreams unfold,
Stories of us, in whispers told.
The compass rose, a guide sincere,
In every beat, your heart I hear.

And as we walk, with courage bold,
Together we will break the mold.
Affinities that time has spun,
Forevermore, we are as one.

Guided by the Stars' Timeless Light

On nights when darkness starts to creep,
The stars awaken, their secrets keep.
With silver beams, they guide our way,
Illuminating dreams at play.

Each twinkle sings of hope and grace,
A cosmic dance in endless space.
Through winding paths and distant shores,
The stars conspire, we find new doors.

In every glimmer, a wish is cast,
Reflections of futures, bright and vast.
With hearts ignited, we soar on high,
Together, beneath this endless sky.

Guided by light that never fades,
In the tapestry of time's cool shades.
We journey on, through night and day,
With stars to show us the way.

Flowing with the Currents of Connection

In whispers soft and shadows near,
We dance through realms of silent cheer.
Hearts beating close, yet worlds apart,
Threads of fate bind every heart.

Waves of laughter, currents strong,
Together weaving, where we belong.
A river flows with stories told,
In every glance, a treasure unfolds.

Hands reach out, in warm embrace,
Time stands still in this sacred space.
Unity in the ebb and flow,
A tapestry where we both glow.

Journeys Beyond the Veil of Time

In dreams we wander, vast and wide,
Through echoes where memories bide.
Stars align in a celestial dance,
Guiding us with a fleeting glance.

Timeless whispers in the breeze,
Carried softly, hearts at ease.
Beyond horizons, secrets fly,
In every heartbeat, a sweet goodbye.

Moments linger in twilight's hue,
Threads of fate weave stories anew.
Together we stand, hand in hand,
Defying the grasp of shifting sand.

Charting the Unknown Realms of Love

With maps of stars and dreams ablaze,
We navigate through life's maze.
Each heartbeat like a compass true,
Guiding paths that lead to you.

Uncharted lands, a daring quest,
In the unknown, we find our nest.
Through storms that rage and skies so clear,
Our love endures, with none to fear.

In every glance and every sigh,
We chart our course through the vast sky.
Love's gentle winds, a soft embrace,
A journey shared, a timeless grace.

In the Wake of Gentle Touches

In shadows cast by morning light,
Soft whispers linger, hearts take flight.
The warmth of hands, a healing grace,
In this moment, we find our place.

Gentle touches, like a sigh,
Echo softly as time flies by.
In tender beats, connections thrive,
In love's embrace, we feel alive.

With every brush, a spark ignites,
Creating dreams in endless nights.
Together woven, souls align,
In the wake of love, divinely entwined.

Portals to Empathy's Abode

In quiet whispers, hearts collide,
A tapestry of feelings wide,
Through portals bright, we see anew,
The world through me, the world through you.

Beneath the weight of hidden tears,
We find the strength to face our fears,
In every story, love ignites,
Bringing us closer on starry nights.

With open arms and gentle grace,
We share the burdens we embrace,
For every soul that longs to share,
In empathy, we're always aware.

Together we step, hand in hand,
A dance of hope across the land,
In empathy's glow, let's reside,
For love resides on every side.

Heartbeats in Rhythm with Nature

The forest hums a soft refrain,
As life awakens after rain,
Each heartbeat syncs with rustling leaves,
In nature's arms, the spirit believes.

The river flows with timeless grace,
It carries dreams to every place,
With every wave, a tale is spun,
In harmony, we are as one.

Mountains stand in silent pride,
The ancient stones, our humble guide,
In every breeze that stirs the air,
We find our peace, a love to share.

Underneath the vast, bright sky,
The stars above in whispers sigh,
In nature's heart, our souls delight,
With every pulse, we find our light.

The Trail of Yesterday's Echoes

Along the path of time we tread,
Where shadows dance, and whispers spread,
Each step a memory left behind,
In echoes lost, our past we find.

The wind carries stories of old,
Of dreams and hopes that once were bold,
In every rustle, secrets speak,
Of heart's desires and futures bleak.

With every footprint in the dust,
We mold our lives, in change we trust,
Remembered laughter, silent cries,
They weave the fabric of our skies.

Through winding roads and trails obscure,
We seek the truth, the heart's allure,
In yesterday's embrace, we glean,
The lessons learned in spaces between.

Unfolding Wings of a New Journey

Beneath the dawn of dreams untold,
We spread our wings, our spirits bold,
With every step, the past is shed,
We rise anew, with faith we're led.

The horizon calls, a path unknown,
With courage strong, we walk alone,
Each moment shines with endless chance,
In the rhythm of our dance.

The winds of change, they softly blow,
Through open hearts, our courage grows,
In every challenge, growth we find,
A tapestry of humankind.

As we embrace the world anew,
With hope as bright as morning dew,
We'll write our stories, fierce and free,
With each new journey, we'll just be.

Spires of Longing Reaching High

Beneath the sky, the towers stand,
Reaching for dreams, a silent command.
Whispers of hope in the evening light,
Echoes of wishes that take flight.

Time drifts like clouds, soft and low,
Spires shine bright in the crimson glow.
Hearts entwined in the twilight's embrace,
Together we wander, a sacred place.

Through the shadows, a symphony plays,
Harmonies linger in golden rays.
In the stillness, our spirits climb,
Bound by the magic, suspend the time.

Of Cloves and Cherries in the Breeze

In the market, sweet scents delight,
Cloves and cherries in soft daylight.
Laughter dances like petals in air,
Moments of joy we choose to share.

Breezes carry whispers of love,
Nature's chorus from skies above.
Every taste holds a story clear,
Filling the heart with memories dear.

Under the branches, we sit in peace,
In this orchard, our worries cease.
With every bite, the world slows down,
Wearing happiness like a crown.

Sketches on the Canvas of Memory

Brush strokes of time paint tales untold,
Fleeting moments in colors bold.
Each scene unfolds like a whispered song,
Captured forever, where we belong.

Faded images, yet bright they gleam,
Scattered visions, remnants of dreams.
In every corner, a laughter hides,
Fragments of joy where love abides.

Ink of nostalgia colors the night,
Sketching our past in silver light.
Under the stars, we reminisce,
Holding each memory, a timeless bliss.

Crisscrossed Paths of Intimacy

Two souls wander through winding trails,
Tangled together, where love prevails.
With every step, the journey grows,
In the heartbeat of life, affection flows.

Secrets whispered beneath the stars,
Crisscrossed paths, both near and far.
With every turn, new stories unfold,
Hand in hand, in the night so bold.

Future dances in the softest light,
Dreams intertwine, pure and bright.
As shadows fade, our hearts align,
In this embrace, forever entwined.

The Labyrinth of Yearning Souls

In shadows deep where whispers dwell,
A maze of dreams, a silent spell.
Hearts wander lost, seeking the light,
Yearning souls in endless night.

Through corridors of hope and pain,
Each winding path a soft refrain.
Together yet apart they roam,
Finding solace far from home.

With every turn, a secret's grace,
In mirrored eyes, they find their place.
A flicker of flame ignites the dark,
A shared desire, a subtle spark.

At last, a bridge of trust is crossed,
In unity, no love is lost.
Through labyrinths of heart and mind,
They seek the truths that they'll find.

Vistas of Shared Solitude

In quiet fields where shadows lay,
Two souls awake to greet the day.
A gentle breeze, a whispered tone,
In solitude, they are not alone.

Mountains rise and valleys fall,
In silence, they hear nature's call.
Together they embrace the still,
In shared quiet, their hearts fulfill.

The horizon stretches wide and free,
A canvas brushed by destiny.
In every glance, a story shared,
In peaceful realms, their spirits bared.

Though lost at times in wanderlust,
They hold the bond of mutual trust.
In the warmth of silent glow,
They find the strength to just let go.

The Threads That Bind Us All

In every stitch, a tale is spun,
Of love and loss, and battles won.
Threads of laughter, threads of tears,
Weaving dreams throughout the years.

Connected hearts in different skies,
Each thread a bond that never dies.
Through trial's test and stormy weather,
In strength and hope, we stand together.

The tapestry of life unfolds,
With colors bright and stories told.
In every knot, a memory held,
In every seam, a truth dispelled.

Together we weave a brighter fate,
In unity, we elevate.
These threads of life that intertwine,
Are signs of love, forever shine.

A Songborne in Solitary Nights

In twilight's hush, a song begins,
A serenade where silence spins.
Beneath the stars, the echoes flow,
In solitude, the heart will grow.

Each note a whisper to the moon,
The melody of life's sweet tune.
In shadows deep where dreams take flight,
A song is born in lonely night.

With every chord, a soul's embrace,
In solitude, they find their place.
Starlit skies, a symphony,
A harmony in unity.

Though solitude may seem so vast,
In song, they find a bond that lasts.
A journey shared in heart and song,
In lonely nights, they both belong.

Treading on Dreams' Embers

Whispers of night cling to the air,
Footprints in ashes, moments we share.
Flickering shadows, a dance with time,
Hearts ignite softly, in rhythm and rhyme.

Shattered reflections, the past calls our name,
Through flickering flames, we rise from the same.
Echoes of laughter, we chase in the dark,
Painting our futures, igniting the spark.

In the silence, hope weaves through the gloom,
Embers of longing burst forth, they bloom.
A tapestry woven with threads of desire,
Each step we take, fuels the fire.

Awake in the twilight, we dream of the dawn,
Through treading on embers, a new path is drawn.
Letting go gently, yet holding on tight,
We dance through our dreams, bathed in soft light.

Mapping Emotional Highways

Routes carved in feelings, winding and true,
Navigating rivers of azure and blue.
Highways of heartbeats, each mile holds a tale,
Through valleys of sorrow, we sail without fail.

Markers of moments, both bitter and sweet,
Detours of laughter where love and loss meet.
Signposts of silence, on journeys we roam,
Seeking connections, we find our way home.

Paths overgrown with the weeds of regret,
Yet blossoms of hope are the paths we reset.
Winding through pathways, we gather our strength,
Mapping emotions, we measure the length.

In this vast landscape, our stories unfold,
Carved with compassion, in warmth not in cold.
Every heartbeat echoes, a road that we've paved,
Mapping emotional highways, each heart we have saved.

Steps Beyond the Veil

Veils of existence, pulled back with a sigh,
Glimmers of truth dance low in the sky.
Each step forward, a bridge to the light,
Revealing the mysteries hidden from sight.

Whispers of shadows, secrets they keep,
Within the stillness, the dreamers leap.
Voices of courage call forth the brave,
Beyond the horizon, new worlds to pave.

In the darkness, we gather our grace,
Holding the silence, we find our own space.
Steps that we take, both cautious and bold,
Beyond the veil, our stories unfold.

With every heartbeat, we venture anew,
Guided by spirits, the old and the true.
Together we wander, hand in hand we sail,
Faced with the stars, we break through the veil.

A Voyage Through Unseen Currents

Sailing on tides of the heart's gentle pull,
Navigating dreams, both vibrant and dull.
Currents of whispers, we drift on the breeze,
Secrets of the ocean, we follow with ease.

Each wave a story, each splash a refrain,
Guided by starlight, we dance through the rain.
With sails of desire, we chart our own course,
Embracing each moment, drawn forth with force.

Beneath the surface, mysteries hide,
In currents unseen, our fears coincide.
Yet through the darkness, the light we will find,
A voyage through waters, both gentle and blind.

With hearts as our compass, we'll never lose track,
Adventurers, seekers, we'll never look back.
Together we journey, with spirits set free,
On a voyage through currents, just you and me.

Undercurrents of Hidden Affection

In shadows soft, where whispers dwell,
A glance exchanged, too shy to tell.
Hearts beat gently, a silent song,
In hidden corners, where we belong.

Soft sighs linger, like morning mist,
Promises hang in the air, unmissed.
Each tender look, a story spun,
In undulating waves, our hearts are one.

Beneath the surface, currents flow,
In quiet moments, love can grow.
Two souls entwined, a dance unseen,
In every heartbeat, what might have been.

Time moves slowly, shadows blend,
In unspoken words, our hearts extend.
With every pulse, a secret shared,
Undercurrents weave, affection bared.

Conversations with the Wind

Whispers in the trees, secrets unfold,
The wind carries stories, both new and old.
It sings through the leaves, a gentle guide,
In the dance of nature, we find our pride.

Clouds drift lazily, thoughts take flight,
Mirroring dreams, both day and night.
Each gust a sigh, each breeze a laugh,
In moments shared, we carve our path.

Echoes of laughter, in open fields,
The touch of the breeze, its warmth reveals.
Carrying wishes, like feathers afloat,
In conversations with wind, our hopes devote.

As twilight whispers, and stars align,
The wind holds secrets, yours and mine.
In every rustle, we find our place,
Embracing the journey, with gentle grace.

Horizons Beyond the Sun's Embrace

Golden hues dance on the ocean's face,
Horizons beckon, in a warm embrace.
Beyond the waves, where dreams take flight,
In the glow of the dawn, we find our light.

Clouds paint stories in vibrant array,
Each sunset whispers the end of the day.
With every color, the sky ignites,
A tapestry woven with radiant sights.

Footprints linger on the soft, warm sand,
In the silence, we make our stand.
Chasing the stars as daylight fades,
In the heart of dusk, our love cascades.

Endless skies call with a promise made,
In the shadows of twilight, we are unafraid.
For horizons stretch far, where dreams reside,
In the sun's embrace, we live, we glide.

The Bridge Between What Was and What Is

In quiet moments, memories flow,
Bridges of time where emotions grow.
Each step taken on paths long paved,
In reflections of past, our hearts are braved.

Echoes of laughter, tender and warm,
Forming connections that weather the storm.
Footprints linger on the edges of time,
In the heart's narrative, love learns to rhyme.

Between the then and the now we find,
A tapestry woven, both gentle and kind.
Each thread a story, a lesson divine,
In the arch of remembrance, our souls entwine.

Held in the balance of what we recall,
In the bridge of existence, we rise and we fall.
For every heartbeat ties us anew,
In the dance of the present, we move through.

Whispers of Affection

In the stillness where shadows play,
Soft words dance on the breeze's sway.
Hearts entwined in secret grace,
A touch, a smile, a warm embrace.

Beneath the stars, our souls ignite,
Whispered vows break through the night.
Laughter echoes, sweet and true,
In every glance, I see you too.

Time stands still in this sacred blend,
Where every moment seems to mend.
Gentle whispers, deep and kind,
For love like this, we seek and find.

In every heartbeat, we remain,
A soft refrain in love's sweet chain.
Bound by warmth, so tenderly,
Whispers of affection set us free.

Journey Through Pulse and Silence

With every beat, we carve our way,
Through stormy nights and vibrant day.
A journey marked by pulse, by breath,
In silence, we dance with life and death.

We wander roads both marked and bare,
In hidden paths, our dreams laid bare.
The silence speaks where words may fail,
In this mystery, we set our sail.

Hands intertwined, we feel the flow,
Of every moment, high and low.
In the pulse of time, we drift and sway,
Guided by heartbeats that won't stray.

Where echoes linger, love takes flight,
In pulse and silence, we find the light.
Forever searching, side by side,
Our journey unfolds, our hearts our guide.

A Map of Hidden Longings

In starlit skies, our secrets lie,
A map of dreams that never die.
With every heartbeat, we seek to know,
The hidden longings that ebb and flow.

Through forests deep and mountains high,
Whispers of hope in the night sky.
Underneath the surface, souls align,
Drawing treasures from the divine.

Lost in thoughts and fleeting chance,
With every glance, we start to dance.
Each longing etched in time and space,
A beautiful game of love's embrace.

Follow the signs where feelings tread,
In the pathways where our spirits wed.
With every heartbeat, we redefine,
The map of hidden longings, yours and mine.

Trail of Beating Dreams

In twilight's glow, our dreams take flight,
On a trail marked by the soft moonlight.
Steps of courage, whispers of grace,
Together we chase in this boundless space.

Through valleys deep and rivers wide,
We find the strength to turn the tide.
With each heartbeat, our spirits bind,
In the rhythm of love, we unwind.

The stars above, a guiding light,
Leading us through the endless night.
Each dream a step, each pulse a sign,
On this winding path, our hearts align.

As dawn breaks forth, we rise anew,
The trail of beating dreams, just us two.
In every moment, we find our way,
Together in love, come what may.

Echoing Dreams Among the Stars

In the stillness of the night,
Whispers dance through velvet skies.
Each star a secret, shining bright,
A tapestry where hope lies.

Chasing shadows, we take flight,
Through realms where wishes gleam.
Guided by the soft moonlight,
We wander in our dreams.

Echoes of laughter, pure and sweet,
Painting galaxies far and wide.
In the cosmic rhythm, hearts meet,
On this celestial ride.

Together we embrace the dark,
Finding solace, lost in space.
For in the quiet, we leave a mark,
In this endless, starry place.

The Shadow of Your Smile

In twilight's gentle embrace,
Your smile casts a warm glow.
A reflection of kindness and grace,
In the moments we both know.

Each laugh a soft lullaby,
Echoing in the chambers of time.
A tender bond, you and I,
In the rhythm of love's rhyme.

When shadows fall and darkness creeps,
I find strength in your light.
It lingers, and softly it keeps,
A beacon through the night.

The warmth of your gaze, so sincere,
Illuminates the paths we tread.
In the silence, you draw me near,
With every word left unsaid.

A Tour Through Celestial Emotions

Embarking on this endless flight,
Across the vast, celestial seas.
With every star, we trace the light,
And sail on whispering dreams.

From the nebula of pure delight,
To the black hole of despair.
Emotions flicker, day and night,
In the cosmic dance we share.

Comets streak through vibrant skies,
Carrying wishes, hopes, and fears.
In this journey, love defies,
The gravity of fleeting years.

Through the universe, hand in hand,
We navigate our hearts' design.
In every corner, we will stand,
Woven in this starry line.

Bridges Built on Shared Moments

Across horizons, we have crossed,
Building bridges, time well spent.
In laughter's echo, never lost,
Memories bloom; our hearts content.

Every tear and every smile,
A cornerstone of what we share.
Through every mile, every trial,
In the journey, love lays bare.

With each moment, stronger ties,
Glimmers of hope within our gaze.
We find strength as time flies,
In the warmth of our shared days.

Together we shall always stand,
Two souls united, brave and true.
With faith, we'll lend a guiding hand,
As bridges join me and you.

Heartstrings Tied in Hope

In the silence of the night,
Dreams whisper soft and bright.
Fingers touch the threads of fate,
Woven tight, it's not too late.

Stars above, they gleam and gleam,
In every heart, a glowing dream.
With every beat, the courage grows,
In hope's embrace, the spirit flows.

Through the storms, we'll find our way,
Guided by the light of day.
Holding tight, we'll never part,
A symphony of every heart.

Solitary Paths of Reflection

Walking softly on this road,
Finding peace in every load.
Shadows dance in fading light,
Guiding thoughts into the night.

Quiet whispers fill the air,
Memories linger, sweet and rare.
Each step taken, wisdom gained,
In solitude, the soul is trained.

Nature speaks, a gentle call,
In stillness, I can feel it all.
Paths might twist, but I won't fear,
For in my heart, the way is clear.

The Language of Glances and Grins

In a crowded space we meet,
A glance shared, so bittersweet.
Unspoken words float through the air,
In every smile, a silent care.

Eyes connect like threads of fate,
Moments linger, never late.
In playful winks, the secrets hide,
In laughter's echo, hearts collide.

While words may falter, love will shine,
In gestures small, our souls entwine.
The silent songs we sing and sway,
Keep the doubts and fears at bay.

Mosaics of Memory and Moments

Fragments of time, like colored glass,
Each a story, none shall pass.
Piecing life in vibrant hues,
In every shard, the joy or blues.

From laughter shared to tears we cry,
In the tapestry, we can't deny.
Moments mingle, love's embrace,
In every crack, a sacred space.

As seasons change, we find our thread,
In the patterns of words unsaid.
Together we create and blend,
A mosaic that will never end.

Milton Keynes UK
Ingram Content Group UK Ltd.
UKHW030751121124
451094UK00013B/793

9 789916 907733